Aji

An IR#4 Business Philosophy

Book One

Book Two

Book Three

Aji

An IR#4 Business Philosophy

Book Three

How to Double Your Income

or Become Rich

in The Fourth Industrial Revolution

TOBY HECHT

Contents

Book Three

Chapter Seven

*****

Contents

Book One

Introduction

    Book One: "*Aji*"

                        *The Strategic and Competitive Differences
Between IR#3 and IR#4*

    Book Two: *Learning and Using "Aji" to Earn a
Living or Become Rich*

    Book Three: *Assignments and Reflection Questions for
Individuals and Networks of Capabilities
to Begin to Increase Their Productivity,
Value and Incomes*

Chapter Four

*****

*****

Contents

Book Two

Without "enough money", it isn't possible for human beings to survive, adapt to life's always changing circumstances, or live a good life.

Chapter Five

The purpose of this chapter is to explain a "competitive, fundamental strategy" so that when you read each of The Strategy's 12 parts in the next chapter

> *... you can learn them effectively, strategically and competitively enough to fulfill your financial, career and business intentions.*

Chapter Six

The Aji Source® Fundamental Strategy's

12 Strategic Intentions

Earning a living for oneself and one's family is the most important, practical and dignified purpose of work for an adult.

Business is practical philosophy in action and competition.

IR#4 Strategic Knowledge replaces the use of IR#3 business knowledge to earn a living or become rich in IR#4.

"Ethics of Power" are *directly*, *explicitly* and *intentionally* competitive.

* The Strategy's "Tactical Pivot"

The Strategy's Tactical Pivot is used to "make money".

* The Strategy's "Strategic Pivot"

The Strategic Pivot is a reliable, robust, strategic and
competitive "Source of Power" in IR#4.

Knowledge and Money ARE Freedom.

The first accomplishments IR#4 businesspeople learn to design
with "Aji" are fresh, new, highly valued and scarce OPNS.

Why are *Superior* Identities, or Gossip, important strategically?

IR#4 Business Leaders *HELP* people fulfill their intentions.

No More "Hot Dog Stands" in IR#4!

Anticipating is all about Time and "Spaces of Possibilities".

Having "time to anticipate" is a fundamental competitive advantage.

*****

Book Three

Introduction

"Aji"

And The Fourth Industrial Revolution (IR#4)

From the book series:

Aji Notes

Strategic Distinctions and Competitive Business Skills

to Double Productivity, Value and Income

(Volumes 1 - 4)

The Fourth Industrial Revolution (IR#4) began in the 1980s when personal computers and, later, the internet came into existence. Since then, businesspeople's computers have become their primary money-making tools.

The problem for businesspeople is that *how* to use their computers strategically and competitively to double their incomes so they can save enough money for 25+ years of old age with their spouse isn't obvious or commonsensical.

When businesspeople use Aji's fundamental strategy and tactics, *the subject of this book series,* they fix this problem.

Together, the strategy and tactics show them how to increase their incomes and savings enough in IR#4 to live a good life until they are at least 90 years old instead of suffering about the future with their spouse because they lack enough savings.

Using Aji -- *The Aji Source Fundamental Strategy* and the four fundamental tactics used to execute it -- shows businesspeople how to increase their competitive capabilities and advantages with their computers so they can double their productivity, value and incomes.

Businesspeople say using Aji to double their incomes and increase their savings for old age is easy, enjoyable and definitive.

It reduces their anxiety about the future, improves their careers and marriages, and opens completely new opportunities to fulfill their financial, career and business ambitions.

* In Chapter One (Book One), I offer a deeper explanation of IR#4, including why IR#3 business skills no longer work in IR#4's complex, rapidly changing and intensely competitive computer-driven global marketplace.

*****

Using This Book Series to Learn and Use "Aji"

To Double Your Income or Become Rich

In The Fourth Industrial Revolution

A Note From The Author

In this book series I explain "Aji" so businesspeople, and entire business organizations, can learn and use it to increase their productivity, value and incomes significantly using the assignments in Chapter Seven.

It's very important Readers keep in mind that "Aji" is a new *business philosophy*.

> It is an entirely new interpretation about business, which means it contains an entirely new set of *ambitions, moods, language, interpretations, distinctions, intentions, commitments* and *practices.*

> *No one understands what they are learning, at first. It's that new.*

I recommend you read and work with the books in the order I wrote them. I wrote them to unfold gradually so new philosophical and business distinctions, concepts and practices are introduced and explained as you need them.

Since "Aji" exists in businesspeople's language before it can be used in the marketplace to increase productivity, value and incomes, I urge Readers to notice and use the new language and practices as much and as often as they can.

If you are a business owner, executive or manager, and you are ready to use "Aji" with your employees, focus on learning The Strategy and the *meanings* of the new language first. Have everyone use them throughout the day, every day.

To help businesspeople I use many of the most fundamental distinctions and practices in "Aji" *recurrently* throughout the book to show how they are used to take care of different business concerns, situations, capabilities and strategies.

I also *repeat* many of them to make explanations, reading and learning easier, and put in lots of white space for note taking.

Occasionally, businesspeople who read to understand instead of to learn, or who are not used to how I write to learn instead of to understand, react to the recurrence, repetition, white space and lists as if they are mistakes or should not be there.

The purpose of each of them is to lower the costs and increase the convenience to learn "Aji" using Chapter Seven.

*****

The Books' Contents

From the Author presents my personal reasons for designing "Aji" and writing the books.

How to Use "Aji" and This Book Series to Produce **Superior** *Outcomes* offers suggestions about how to use the books to learn the philosophy's new strategic and competitive *intentions* and *business skills*.

*****

Book One

"Aji"

Chapter One, "Aji, An IR#4 Business Philosophy", presents the books' intentions for individual businesspeople and for business owners, executives and managers.

It explains that to earn a living or become rich in IR#4 requires new *strategic intentions* and *tactical business skills,* different from those sufficient to earn a high IR#3 income. This new set of intentions and skills is called "Aji".

It explains the consequences to IR#3 businesspeople who do not "pivot" away from IR#3's practices and toward IR#4's, the consequences if they do "pivot" with "Aji", why IR#3 business skills no longer work, and the proof that "Aji" enables the production of top 1% incomes.

Chapter Two previews *The Aji Source Fundamental Strategy.*

It contains a one-page version of *The Aji Source Fundamental Strategy* and a longer *high-level "Preview" version.*

Together they begin to explain the new *ambitions, moods, language, distinctions, interpretations, intentions, commitments, practices* and *outcomes* used in "Aji" to produce much higher IR#4 Incomes.

The Strategic and Competitive Differences

Between IR#3 and IR#4

Chapter Three explains *two fundamental differences* between
IR#3 and IR#4 that present The Big Picture.

It explains how businesspeople in IR#3 were able to make the
parts of their lives and careers a unified whole to fulfill their
intentions -- called "operational coherence" -- using processes
and procedures.

In IR#4 businesspeople must accomplish operational
coherence by making sure every part of every specific action
plan they design and execute works together as a unified
whole -- called *"strategic coherence"* -- using "Aji", not
processes and procedures.

This lets businesspeople see that learning how to use their
computers and the internet to make very high incomes
requires new thought and action that is challenging,
meaningful, interesting, stimulating and dignified.

Chapter Three also explains the nature and operations of IR#4's
rapidly changing, complex, intensely competitive and
technologically advanced competitive situations compared to
IR#3's slower-paced world.

Chapter Four explains *six practical, strategic* and *competitive differences* between IR#3 and IR#4:

1. The *tools* businesspeople use in IR#4 to produce competitive advantages, superior value and very high incomes are radically different.

2. The *strategic* and *tactical skills*, or the business *knowledge*, needed to compete successfully in IR#4 are different.

3. Understanding *"real"* money is essential to earn much higher IR#4 Incomes.

4. *Adult dignity* is important for *making money* in IR#4 and *making money* is important for *adult dignity.*

5. *Work ethics* in IR#4 are different and are called *Ethics of Power.*

6. *Careers, or Identities*, are different in IR#4.

Book Two

Learning and Using "Aji"

To Earn a Living or Become Rich

Chapter Five explains what a competitive, fundamental strategy such as *The Aji Source Fundamental Strategy* is, how it is organized, how it works and how to use it with the business skills (*IR#4 Strategic Knowledge*) needed to execute it.

The Strategy is a Master Plan for designing specific competitive strategies. The chapter includes the *12 Competitive Design Concerns* and *5 Properties* IR#4 businesspeople use to design competitive strategies.

This is helpful for businesspeople in their personal careers when they are beginning to learn how to use "Aji" to change their task orientation to a strategic and competitive one.

It's helpful for business owners, executives and managers when they begin to use "Aji" to pivot their business organizations towards IR#4 so they can fulfill their financial, career and business intentions.

Chapter Six presents an explanation of each of the 12 parts of The Strategy that businesspeople can use to get started in their career and/or business.

It explains each of The Strategy's 12 *strategic intentions* in some depth and gives some of the tactics (*IR#4 Strategic Knowledge*) needed to begin to execute it.

Book Three

Assignments and Reflection Questions

For Individuals and Networks of Capabilities

To begin to increase their productivity, value and incomes

Chapter Seven contains two assignments that enable businesspeople to use the books to learn "Aji" individually or with Networks of Capabilities to begin increasing their productivity, value and incomes.

The first assignment helps *individuals* use the books to pivot.

The second assignment helps *Networks of Capabilities*, or entire business organizations, work together in person or online anywhere in the world to learn and use "Aji".

*****

About the Author

Toby Hecht is founder of The Aji Network, a business education company that, for over 30 years in a complex, rapidly changing and intensely competitive computer-driven global marketplace, has championed businesspeople's ability to "earn a living" with annual incomes between $400k and $4m. He is a businessman, as well as a teacher and student of philosophy, history and linguistics; business and leadership; military strategy and martial arts. He has been a top 1% performer for decades.

Following graduation from Tulane University, he moved to California where he and his wife and business partner, Linda, started their business careers. Together, they have founded and operated three successful companies.

Mr. Hecht began writing in his 30s when he set out to read, deconstruct and summarize common knowledge found in more than 60 classic business texts used in courses offered by Stanford University. He used what he learned to begin writing and teaching uncommon, "strategic knowledge" needed to perform in the top 1% of a newly evolving, computer-driven, knowledge-based economy.

Mr. Hecht served as "key faculty" at General Electric's Crotonville Business School, the #1 corporate business school in the country, for six years and consistently ranked as the top instructor in his field. He consulted several businesses that subsequently sold, earning the owners $8m to $30m.

In the 30 years since he founded The Aji Network, his third business, he has taught nearly 4,000 ambitious businesspeople how to compete for and earn annual incomes, capital-at-work and enterprise values that are high enough to enable them to live a good life throughout their entire lives, including 25+ years of unemployment during their old age.

He is the designer and principal teacher of The Aji Network's courses, programs, workshops and conferences. He has authored more than 1300 papers, produced more than 400 talks and lead over 350 conferences aimed exclusively at enabling students of The Aji Network to earn annual incomes of $400k to $4m.

He is also author of *Aji, An IR#4 Business Philosophy*, a three-book series, and *Aji Notes: Strategic Distinctions and Competitive Business Skills to Double Productivity, Value and Income*, a four-volume series.

Today, Mr. Hecht lives on a ranch in California with his wife and dogs, and continues to design, write and teach for The Aji Network.

*****

From The Author

Why "Aji"?

The focus of my career for almost 40 years has been on earning a living or becoming rich in The Fourth Industrial Revolution (IR#4) for the sake of being able to survive, adapt to life's always changing circumstances and live a good life with my family. I've fulfilled my intentions by helping over 4,000 businesspeople fulfill the same intentions for their families.

In a marketplace full of loud, political, competing, shallow, misleading, obvious, angry, cynical, disingenuous and often meaningless arguments about what should be important to businesspeople, earning "enough money" to fulfill my marriage vows and commitments to my children has been my ideological and moral center.

My business philosophy and my businesses have always been a *practical* manifestation of the vows I made to my wife, Linda, the day we married, and later of the commitments we both made to avoid becoming a financial burden on our children and their spouses when they became adults. Nothing else makes sense to me.

How could I let someone I care about deeply, whom I'd promised to love, honor and cherish in front of our families and friends, and who gave me her trust, casually face a future in which she and I would run out of money during our old age?

How could I raise children and then thoughtlessly compel them and their spouses to support Linda and me, reducing their ability to take care of their own children?

This may sound corny, simplistic or hopelessly naïve to people who feel there are more important and sophisticated intellectual, social, entertaining or political agendas than earning and saving enough money to live a good life with my wife while raising our children *and* during our old age.

But I'm unapologetically simpleminded and idealistic when it comes to taking care of my wife and children. It's what I promised them I'd do. It's my most important, practical and dignified commitment. It gives my life meaning.

From my childhood memories, as well as my common sense, I know that real life without enough money is harsh, inescapable and miserable, and not an adolescent, television or political fantasy that can be ignored, trivialized or dismissed.

When people run out of money, *practical breakdowns* and *chronic financial stresses* grab hold of them, dominate them, wear them down, trigger despair, thwart their intentions, make them sick and ruin their lives.

Without "enough money" it isn't possible for human beings to survive, adapt to life's always changing circumstances or live a good life, especially when they are old. They can't afford the goods and services we all need to take care of our most fundamental human concerns, such as housing, food, medical care, transportation, family, play and dignity.

Many businesspeople, reporters and politicians act as if this claim can be denied or ignored and isn't important enough to speak about. They act as if businesspeople and their spouses can somehow live good lives without burdening their children or suffering chronic financial stresses in their 70s, 80s and 90s when they run out of money.

The claim is the truth.

Knowing this made it impossible for Linda and me to ignore the consequences of any business or financial actions that would thwart our intentions to earn enough income to take practical care of our children and ourselves. And it drove us to learn so we could increase our competitive advantages, productivity, value, income and savings.

Even in our twenties we began to realize the financial actions we would have to take throughout our careers to earn and save "enough money" to avoid betraying our commitments.

When we met with our accountant at that time, the truth about how much money we really needed to earn *and* save began to unfold. We took a big gulp as she told us the financial truths we faced without a pension if we wanted to live a good life together until we were at least 90 years old.

She said we needed to save at least 20% of our pre-tax income in after-tax dollars just to get started, which meant we had to save roughly 50% of every paycheck. Then she told us we'd need to readjust our thinking after we had children. Yikes!

The new financial obligations the IR#4 marketplace had produced were a real shock to both of us, of course. We were raised in The Third Industrial Revolution (IR#3) "to get a job" and use hard work, determination and common sense to earn a living, end of story. After we got a good job everything was supposed to simply work out as we wanted it to.

Neither of us was raised to be financially responsible for our old age. Because no one ever spoke about this financial obligation, we never saw it coming.

Despite the shock, it did not occur to us to deny the truth. Denying it to have what we wanted when we were young and strong in favor of running out of money when we were old and weak seemed absurd, immature and undignified.

What would we say to one another when the moment of truth arrived as the math predicted it would? What would we say to our children and their spouses the day we ran out of money?

Where was the dignity for a married couple, or any adult, in pretending to be "fine" financially when we were not yet able to earn or save enough money to live a good life together our entire life?

Our commitment to deal responsibly with our newly discovered financial situation produced deep and real adult meanings for our finances, marriage, parenting, careers and businesses. At the same time it stressed us.

It meant our conversations together and with our friends and business colleagues, including customers and investors, were real, practical, adult and responsible.

This made them deeply meaningful, which mattered to us, rather than shallow, immature, irresponsible, superficial, full of entertaining, political and intellectual distractions, and certain to produce suffering for everyone in the future.

Later we discovered that our willingness to accept and deal with financial realities honestly, honorably using our best efforts, and straightforwardly without pretention, produced respect and admiration with our children, which was also very important to us.

It's no surprise to any of us that the baby boomers who blew off their financial, marital and familial obligations are the generation most disliked by their children, are divorcing in record numbers and face a future in which they are certain to run out of money before they die if they live a normal lifespan.

We saw this coming and didn't want to be part of it.

To our surprise, our seriousness created a group of friends and customers who were equally serious and unable to tolerate denying their financial obligations to their spouse and children.

To our even greater surprise, simply having character to accept the truth about our financial situation and dealing with it practically as best we could and with dignity produced a degree of trustworthiness, value, authority and leadership that created competitive advantages and opportunities to make a great deal of money with these friends and customers.

Now they, too, are rich and very, very happy about it.

Shortly after we opened the first chain of retail computer stores in Silicon Valley I found myself in the situation I invented "Aji" to solve. I needed to earn a living. I had to use my computer to do it. And, I was clueless about how to think about it.

I had two advantages that helped me solve the problem.

First, it was easy for me to see that businesspeople who had degrees in computer science and used mainframe computers to help businesses make money bought their personal computers "strategically", which is how they had to use them in order to make money for their employers.

They knew how to choose the computer and software programs that could best help them design and execute action plans to build their businesses and make money.

And, second, it was just as easy to see that regular businesspeople with no knowledge of computers whose orientation was task-oriented, labor-based and commonsensical would never be able to compete against the "strategists" successfully. How could they when they thought learning how to operate their new software programs was "cool" and all they needed to learn?

But it wasn't until the internet appeared that I began to have the insights I needed to see how to exploit personal computers' strategic and competitive possibilities.

I've already spoken about *the first insight*:

> Businesspeople can't count on employers and the government to be responsible for their survival the last 25+ years of their lives, as they did in IR#3. Now businesspeople are responsible for funding their old age, as Linda and I recognized almost 40 years ago.

> Businesspeople need to accept that the *meaning* of "earning a living" has changed in IR#4. This change requires them to learn new ideas and skills to be able to succeed.

>> Adults who are serious about taking care of their spouse and children need to change their thinking and practices immediately to increase their productivity, value and incomes to include saving enough money to afford 25+ years of unemployment during their old age.

>> The longer they delay learning how to increase their incomes, the harder it becomes every day to recover.

To survive, adapt to changing circumstances and live a good life with their spouse throughout their entire life in IR#4, businesspeople need to earn *and* save enough money during their 40-year careers to afford the goods and services we all need until we are at least 85-90 years old.

The math to calculate how much money is enough to afford 25 years of old age with one's spouse is so simple and compelling Linda and I just assumed everyone we told would thank us because it would help them avoid suffering, chronic financial stresses and despair later in their life.

Nope. But we found the integrity, courage and commitment of the businesspeople who did thank us very appealing.

The second insight makes *strategic* and competitive sense of computers and the internet but is a bit difficult to grasp at first because the philosophy and concepts needed to explain it are new, and because they only work with computers and the internet.

They are not difficult to learn, but they are a very, very different way of thinking about how to make money in IR#4.

They form the basis of "Aji", which is a business philosophy whose intent is to help businesspeople earn a living or become rich in IR#4 to take care of their families.

I call the philosophy "Aji" after the term used in the 4,000-year-old game of strategy, Go, to mean "having the potential to win". (I explain more about "Aji" in the introduction to the book.)

The second insight is this:

> "Regular businesspeople" -- business owners, executives, managers and individuals -- can and must learn how to exploit the new *strategic* and competitive possibilities computers and the internet bring into existence to earn a living or become rich in the same ways large global competitors do, such as Apple, Amazon, Facebook, Microsoft and Google.

>> Everyone with a computer is now free technologically to design and execute *their own* fresh, new, highly valued and scarce offers, practices, narratives and strategies, including goods and services, to fulfill their financial, career and business intentions.

>> For the first time in history businesspeople have a tool they can carry with them wherever they go and use autonomously, *strategically* and competitively to increase their competitive advantages, productivity, value, incomes and savings, and fulfill their new financial obligations.

To use computers and the internet to compete successfully, businesspeople also need to have a competitive fundamental strategy and the strategic knowledge to execute it *effectively, strategically* and *competitively.*

> I began inventing "Aji's" two components, (1) *The Aji Source Fundamental Strategy* and (2) *The IR#4 Strategic Knowledge* needed to execute it, shortly after opening our computer stores in Silicon Valley. I have been refining them for the past 30 years.

We have shown for decades, and with thousands of businesspeople, that they can double their incomes if they learn "Aji", or how to execute a competitive, fundamental strategy

... and quit using IR#3's labor-based business knowledge, task-oriented work ethics and reliance on common sense.

"Aji" has helped Linda and me meet our financial obligations many times over. As businesspeople in our networks began to see how well Linda and I were doing financially, they began to ask us to help them meet their financial intentions and aspirations.

We were happy to tell them about "Aji", or how to use their computers and the internet *strategically* and competitively, instead of with task orientation.

They never expected to hear what I told them about a completely new business philosophy that enables businesspeople to compete successfully in the top 1% of the marketplace to produce incomes between $400k-$4m and that only works with computers and the internet.

Their financial, career and business success using the philosophy formed the foundation for our next business, The Aji Network, where over the past 30 years we've helped thousands of businesspeople take care of their spouse and children meaningfully and with adult dignity.

I hope you can use "Aji" to help you take care of your family, too.

*****

How to Use "Aji" and This Book Series

To Produce Superior Outcomes

The Aji Source Fundamental Strategy is the first of two components that constitute "Aji". It includes the twelve new *strategic intentions* that computers and the internet make possible and that have never existed because businesspeople lacked the tools needed to produce the possibility.

Businesspeople learn this component first.

You will find three different versions of The Strategy in these books and two assignments you can use to learn "Aji" and build your Networks of Capabilities at the same time:

#1 - Use the *one-page version* in Chapter Two (Book One) or Chapter Six (Book Two) to see The Strategy at a glance and to stay oriented in the sequence when you read the longer versions.

#2 - Use the *high-level Preview version*, also in Chapter Two, to begin to learn the strategic intentions of The Strategy's 12 parts and their meanings.

#3 - Use the *longer version* in Chapter Six (Book Two) to begin using The Strategy and learning some of the new tactics, or *IR#4 Strategic Knowledge*, needed to fulfill The Strategy's intentions for your networks of colleagues, employees, employers, vendors and customers, and yourself.

#4 - Use the two assignments in Chapter Seven to learn "Aji" and build your Networks of Capabilities at the same time.

You and your colleagues, employees, employers, vendors and customers can *begin using the knowledge in the three books immediately, or at any time,* to execute The Strategy to increase your productivity and value, and theirs,

> *... by using the recommendations, assignments and instructions in Chapter Seven.*

The many bite-sized pieces of *IR#4 Strategic Knowledge* in this book series, the second component of "Aji", will help you begin to produce these *superior* outcomes:

Earn very high IR#4 Incomes

Think and act effectively, strategically and competitively enough to produce tactical, strategic and fundamental competitive advantages and use them to increase productivity and value

Produce steady streams of highly valued and scarce (1) *offers*, (2) *practices*, (3) *narratives*, (4) *strategies* and (5) *accomplishments* that can be used strategically with Networks of Capabilities

Establish identities of *superior* trustworthiness, value, authority and leadership

Hold highly compensated leadership roles

Build competitive business organizations

Anticipate future competitive threats, obligations and opportunities

*****

The Aji Source® Fundamental Strategy's

12 Strategic Intentions

Part #1: Constitute Life, Financial and Business Ambitions

Part #2: Formulate Philosophies of Care and Competition

Part #3: Accumulate IR#4 Strategic Knowledge

Part #4: Act with Ethics of Power

Part #5: Design and execute a steady stream of fresh, new Offers, Practices, Narratives and Strategies

* The Strategy's "Tactical Pivot"

Part #6: Build IR#4 Networks of Capabilities

* The Strategy's "Strategic Pivot" *begins*

Part #7: Increase Autonomies, or freedoms

Part #8: Produce *highly* valued Accomplishments

Part #9: Establish Identities of *superior* trustworthiness, value, authority and leadership

Part #10: Hold *highly* compensated Leadership Roles

Part #11: Build *competitive* Business Organizations

Part #12: Anticipate *future* Threats, Obligations and Opportunities

Chapter Seven

How to Use This Book Series

To Pivot Towards "Aji"

New

Ambitions, Moods, Language,

Distinctions, Interpretations, Intentions,

Commitments, Practices And Outcomes

That Are Fresh, New, Highly Valued and Scarce

This Chapter contains *two assignments* and instructions you can use to "pivot" towards "Aji" using this book, along with Books One and Two, either (#1) individually or (#2) while building your Network of Capabilities.

Your Network of Capabilities is the array of colleagues, employers, employees, vendors and customers who share your intentions to earn a living or become rich and with whom you learn, think, design, plan and work using "Aji" to fulfill these purposes:

Increase your competitive capabilities and advantages, productivity and value

Earn much higher IR#4 Incomes

Produce steady streams of fresh, new offers, practices, narratives and strategies that are highly valued and scarce relative to demand that you can use *strategically* to execute The Strategy in order to fulfill your financial, career and business intentions

The assignments and instructions are a new way of thinking and orienting, or being, in the marketplace that enables businesspeople to exploit the new strategic and competitive capabilities made possible by computers and the internet.

These capabilities are a new IR#4 business philosophy, "Aji".

No one understands what they are learning, or why it works, when they first begin. Remember, "Aji" is new. It isn't obvious or common sense. What you read won't be familiar. It makes sense in a new way that is made possible using computers and the internet.

Just follow the instructions and allow it to unfold. It will. The descriptions, meanings, relevance, value and purposes of "Aji" build on themselves as you move through the book.

To make yourself and/or your business competitive enough in IR#4 to fulfill your financial, career and business intentions, you will be doing assignments like this, or thinking this way, and having others do them with you, for the rest of your career.

The interpretations and practices used in the assignments are not IR#3 business knowledge or work ethics, or anything like them.

Businesspeople use them to increase their competitive capabilities, productivity, value and incomes effectively, strategically and competitively, not to "get the job done". And they use them to help entire businesses fulfill their financial and business intentions.

When you "pivot", you and your networks learn new *ambitions, moods, language, distinctions, interpretations, intentions, commitments, practices* and *outcomes*.

To use this book to "pivot" -- individually or while building your Networks of Capabilities at the same time -- use one or both assignments that follow.

The first one enables businesspeople who do not have a network and are not in a position to build one to pivot themselves so they can open, or reopen, their future in IR#4 and build their network later.

The second one enables businesspeople and entire businesses to get started using "Aji" to build their Networks of Capabilities -- colleagues, employees, employers, vendors and customers -- at the same time they pivot themselves.

*****

Learn The Strategy by Using The Strategy

In these two assignments you will learn and practice *three learning practices* you can use individually and with your networks for the rest of your career to learn "anything", i.e., (1) recurrence, (2) reciprocation and (3) recursion.

> You will use them purposefully every day, all day, whenever you need to learn "anything", which is essential when you are working to earn a living or become rich in the most rapidly changing, complex, competitive and technologically advanced marketplace in history.

Deep in IR#3 business philosophy lies the notion that the way to learn business knowledge is to use the practices most of us learned in school, which are unpleasant, coercive, meaningless, arbitrary, political, impractical and ineffective.

> In other words, most businesspeople I work with have learned from school to associate education, or learning, with having knowledge imposed on them, suffering and thinking a lot, rather than learning how to think and act with meaning that is satisfying, powerful, gentle and enjoyable.

Consequently, the majority of businesspeople avoid "education" or learning, and I don't blame them. I didn't like being shoved around and coerced into learning, either, especially by teachers who don't actually use or know what they are teaching.

> The marketplace sometimes tries to counter this by attempting to make learning fun or a form of entertainment, which is just as ineffective and undignified for an adult.

With "Aji" you will learn that what you learn is practical, meaningful, relevant, important, useful, worthwhile and "on purpose" for living a good life with one's family, or it isn't worth learning.

This is the same for how you learn. It's either part of living a good life, or it's not worth doing.

To get started …

5 ways to think about learning "Aji"

Use these instructions to begin to orient yourself to learn "Aji".

#1 - *Learn any way you'd like that's* **practical** and **effective.**

> The more you know and/or invent different ways of learning that use the three fundamental learning practices that follow, the better.

> Your nervous system likes *variety* and *recurrence.*

> It doesn't like and will resist *repetition.*

Use the three practices that follow -- which I explain in more detail in the section *"How to Learn ... Anything"* towards the end of this chapter -- to satisfy your nervous system's requirements to learn anything.

They can be used and combined in many different ways, and need to be, because our nervous systems enjoy and respond to different learning situations.

You can use them while sitting in a chair reading, in meetings or while making a presentation.

They make it possible to teach entire business organizations to learn "Aji" gently, easily, skillfully, effectively, strategically, competitively and fluently.

The best way by far to learn effectively and with enjoyment is to use the three practices every day, all day, in real-life competitive situations.

1. *Recurrence:*   Practice speaking and executing The Strategy regularly and in different ways throughout the day, every day, and never stop.

Look for and make opportunities to do this on purpose throughout the day so that you continually improve your interpretations.

2. *Reciprocation:*   Notice and observe the outcomes that come back to you, or that you produce, when you act, all day, every day, individually or with your networks.

Do this deliberately throughout the day, too.

3. *Recursion:* Deepen the *meanings* of what you are learning by speaking improved interpretations about them with your Networks of Capabilities throughout the day.

Do this with colleagues whenever possible.

Then improve your design and/or execution.

What do the outcomes you are producing mean about how you are being in the marketplace and what you are doing? (Are you *being* too busy or *distracted* to be serious about learning and earning a much higher income, or are you *being* serious and dignified?)

How can you use your interpretations to improve how you are thinking and acting to fulfill your ambitions?

These three practices are not difficult to understand or perform.

In addition to being effective, strategic and competitive, they are gentle, sensible, enjoyable and extremely easy to practice whenever you want or need to.

Once you learn them, you "own" them. They are an essential "Source of Power" in IR#4.

#2 - ***Execute The Strategy*** by learning to (1) *speak*, (2) *write* and (3) *fulfill* each of its 12 strategic intentions ***in sequence***.

If you only read, think or try to understand The Strategy, you will not increase your value or income; so don't do it.

Write about it, speak about it and *execute* each part every day. Talk about the whole strategy and the DMRVP of each of its parts to anyone who is interested.

Then, do it again but do it better and never, ever, stop improving your interpretations, designs, practices and outcomes.

Simply learning each of The Strategy's 12 strategic intentions and meanings,

… and then beginning to work on them in sequence to begin to make money,

… "pivots" businesspeople's thoughts and actions *strategically* to naturally and spontaneously begin to quit using task orientation.

This changes the *meaning* of "everything", really.

* * * * *

#3 - ***Begin to use The Strategy as a whole*** to produce competitive capabilities and advantages, and to increase productivity, value and high IR#4 Incomes.

Eventually, you will learn to execute all 12 parts all day, every day, as opportunities appear in meetings or competitive situations, for example, or as you produce them.

This enables you to make *progress* throughout the day to *advance action* needed to increase your productivity, value and income, which was not possible in IR#3 when using single-purpose tools.

At first businesspeople tend to use The Strategy simply by focusing on fulfilling one intention at a time throughout the day.

They go to a meeting and build their *networks*, make a presentation and see how to establish *identities* of superior trustworthiness, value, authority and leadership, or learn a new way to design a highly valued and scarce *offer* with a colleague on the internet.

As businesspeople learn The Strategy they begin to see and invent ways to fulfill more than one strategic intention at a time.

They build their networks and hold a leadership role at the same time, for instance.

Eventually businesspeople learn to see how to invent and make "full moves" throughout the day,

> ... fulfilling all strategic intentions easily, effectively and fluently

> ... to produce competitive advantages and increase their productivity, value and incomes.

>> * To make a "full move" is an expression in the game of Go meaning to take action that serves the best set of strategic and competitive purposes possible in a given competitive situation, such as fulfilling all 12 strategic intentions in a single meeting.

People who see or hear IR#4 businesspeople working with "Aji" can tell they know what they are doing and enjoy their skill.

> Using "Aji", or doubling one's productivity and value so that it works with computers and the internet, is not subtle.

> It's a new set of tactical, strategic and competitive skills that includes new words, and ideas that are strategic and directly competitive.

> Those around you will notice the difference.

#4 - ***Diagnose breakdowns, weaknesses, failures and sources of thwarted intentions*** by going backwards through The Strategy.

This is an effective way to learn The Strategy, too.

It is especially effective for business owners, executives and managers. It enables them to make practical sense of employees' and colleagues' strategic and competitive failures and weaknesses, and show people the tactical and strategic knowledge they need to learn to correct or improve them very quickly.

For instance, if you or someone in your network is dissatisfied with the leadership roles you are able to hold, which is **Part #10** of The Strategy, look backwards at **Part #9** to see if your identities of *superior* trustworthiness, value, authority and leadership exist and are sufficient.

If they aren't, look back at **Part #8** to see if you are producing steady streams of accomplishments that are scarce and valuable enough.

If they aren't, look backward at **Part #7** to see if you have sufficient autonomies to produce highly valued and scarce accomplishments, or if you are working too hard and being too busy to learn, design and produce them.

If you don't have sufficient autonomies, look backward at **Part #6** to see if the Networks of Capabilities you have built are strategic and competitive enough to help you compete successfully.

If they aren't, look backward at *Part #5* to see if you are able to design and execute steady streams of fresh, new, highly valued and scarce offers, practices, narratives and strategies needed to attract and build Networks of Capabilities.

If you aren't, look backward at *Parts #2 - #4* to see if you have the philosophy, knowledge and ethics needed to produce fresh, new OPNS.

If you don't, look backward at *Part #1* to make sure your Life, Financial and Business Ambitions, or your financial, career and business intentions, are well-grounded, deeply meaningful to you and mobilize your thoughts and actions.

#5 - ***Deconstruct and Anticipate competitors' offers, practices, narratives and strategies using The Strategy*** to produce competitive advantages and to increase your competitive capabilities.

Deconstruct their OPNS to better design your own.

Anticipate the OPNS your competitors will design next to be able to counter their moves and/or be "first to market" with yours.

*****

The Pivot Plan

For Individuals

And Building Networks of Capabilities

Here is a plan you and your networks can use with the book and the assignments to "pivot" your business skills so you can think and act effectively, strategically and competitively enough to fulfill your financial, career and business intentions, and produce much higher IR#4 Incomes.

It is spread over 24 weeks, or 168 days.

Since you will need to skip holidays and accommodate vacations, it might take a bit longer.

If you need to learn The Strategy quickly, or immediately, in order to join a Network of Capabilities, you can begin The Plan at Week #13.

To learn "Aji" you must fulfill your nervous system's requirements to learn "anything". There are no shortcuts or exceptions. Your nervous system is a mechanism. Learn how to "play" it enjoyably and powerfully as if it were a musical instrument.

If you don't accept this and decline to use the practices listed below, you will not learn and/or you will begin to forget whatever you understand in two days.

This means your *ambitions* and *moods* need to be effective, strategic and competitive when you work with the assignments, rather than labor-based and task-oriented.

It means you need to *practice recurrence, reciprocation and recursion, every day, all day,* which I explain in greater detail at the end of this chapter.

To enable your nervous system to learn and work as you intend, schedule your meetings weekly and do not stop until you are complete. (It's OK to skip a few weeks for holidays and vacations, but that's all.)

If you stop and start, or people miss *any* meeting, you will interrupt your "recurrence" and trip over yourselves, irritate and offend one another, produce distrust, thwart your intentions to learn "Aji" and find yourselves in bad moods.

When businesspeople are *ambitious* enough to be serious about living a good life,

> … in *wonder* about all there is to learn,

> … *enthusiastic* about the work they need to do,

> … and *passionate* about the future they are producing,

> … the seriousness and discipline required to *double* their incomes to be able to take care of their family is not a problem.

Since this is a new "way of being" in the marketplace, or an entirely different way of orienting, what to do and how to do it needs to be spoken explicitly.

Recurrence, reciprocation and recursion are essential and fundamental learning practices in IR#4.

Using all three of them is necessary to learn and increase your relative capabilities to compete successfully.

Please notice that on Weeks #4 & #14 you read Chapter Six, Part #1: Constitute *your* Life, Financial and Business Ambitions,

... and write them down with your spouse.

Here's a 24-week plan:

Week #1: From the Author and About the Book Series

Week #2: Chapter One

Week #3: Chapter Two: Preview Version of The Strategy

   * *All in Book One*

Week #4: Chapter Six: Part #1, Constitute your Life, Financial and Business Ambitions (Book Two)

To orient yourself to the practice, read and write down your Life, Financial and Business Ambitions the first time after discussing them and the consequences of failure with your spouse.

Call it a rough sketch if you'd like. Be sure you know your Financial and Savings Gaps, and their meanings to your family and you, for the rest of your assignment.

It's all right to begin using the assignments here if you are under pressure to join a Network of Capabilities.

Week #13: Chapter Five

Week #14:   Chapter Six: Part #1, Constitute your Life,
            Financial and Business Ambitions

            Revisit your ambitions with your spouse. Re-write
            them if you need to.

            Deepen and refresh them so they are meaningful to
            both of you. Be clear about the consequences of
            failure.

Week #15: Chapter Six: Part #2

Week #16: Chapter Six: Part #3

Week #17: Chapter Six: Part #4

Week #18: Chapter Six: Part #5

Week #19: Chapter Six: Part #6

Week #20: Chapter Six: Parts #7 & #8

Week #21: Chapter Six: Part #9

Week #22: Chapter Six: Part #10

Week #23: Chapter Six: Part #11

Week #24: Chapter Six: Part #12

   * *All in Book Two*

* * * * *

Aji Assignment Instructions

For Individuals

"Aji" is an IR#4 business philosophy.

It enables businesspeople to *roughly double their productivity, value and incomes* using their computers, the internet and Networks of Capabilities

Its purpose is to make it possible for businesspeople to earn a living, or become rich, in IR#4, which is the most rapidly changing, competitive, complex and technologically advanced global marketplace in history.

This includes enabling business owners, executives and managers to pivot their business organizations so they can fulfill their financial, career and business intentions.

It is a new set of *ambitions, moods, language, distinctions, interpretations, intentions, commitments, practices* and *outcomes* that can only be used with computers and the internet.

As you learn "Aji", you will learn how to use them effectively, strategically and competitively enough to fulfill your financial intentions, or to produce a high IR#4 Income.

Use this *Aji Assignment* to "pivot" towards using "Aji" to fulfill your financial, career and business intentions.

If you do not have a Network of Capabilities with whom you will work with the book -- yet -- use only this assignment until you do. Then get to work building!

If you are building and working with a network, use this assignment in between your weekly meetings to prepare for them.

When working on the assignment *take care of yourself* as if you are in a serious, long-term competition because you are. Don't abuse yourself or beat yourself up in any way.

Make sure you have a comfortable and quiet place to sit, read, take notes, write and/or speak with your colleagues.

Make sure your space is neat, clean and uncluttered.

Have a drink that you enjoy handy, such as coffee or tea, and snacks.

If playing music helps you focus and manage your mood, play it.

Continue to redesign and improve your work space and practices as you get the hang of learning "Aji".

In IR#4, learning is part of everyone's career and business, and part of living a good life. Learn how to learn in ways that work for you and with colleagues you enjoy and respect. Don't suffer.

*****

Assignment Questions

For Individuals

A. *Always manage your moods first.*

Read the section "Manage your moods when you learn The Strategy" before answering these questions. It's the last section of this chapter.

1. What was your mood when you began reading the section of the book you will work with this week?

   Were you, for example, dreading having to do the assignment, excited about it, flat and disinterested, curious or enthusiastic?

2. What was your mood when you finished your reading?

3. What is your mood now as you start answering the questions in this assignment?

*****

The purpose of these questions is to begin to develop your ability to notice, observe and assess your moods, and the moods of businesspeople in your networks.

As you learn to observe moods, you begin to "see" that people's moods predetermine what they are willing and able to learn, think or act. They are precursors to success and failure.

One reason IR#3 businesspeople have trouble learning to pivot is their moods are labor-based, busy and hardworking, task-oriented or focused on getting the job done, and nonchalant about relying on their common sense to figure out what to do.

"Bad Moods" shut down learning, design, strategic thinking and competitive action. They prevent businesspeople from building competitive Networks of Capabilities.

They include being skeptical, cynical or distrustful automatically, or for no reason, which is unattractive, drives up costs and is uncompetitive.

They also include being in despair, resigned, panicked, entitled, greedy, "wonderful", naive, argumentative, small-minded, closed-minded, prideful, petty, arrogant, conceited, trivializing, "shitty", mean-spirited, positional and rigid.

"Good Moods" open, launch or advance strategic thinking and competitive action. They enable businesspeople to build global Networks of Capabilities and earn high IR#4 Incomes.

They include *ambition, humility, prudence, dignity, responsibility, curiosity, interest, wonder* about all there is to learn, *enthusiasm* for the work that needs to be done and *passion* for the future you are producing for yourself and your family.

B. *Always manage your financial, career and business intentions second*

4. What is your Savings Gap? What is your Income Gap?

Your *"Savings Gap"* is the difference between the amount of money you need to accumulate (the result of saving and passively investing) by your 60th birthday and the amount you actually have saved.

You need "enough savings" to avoid running out of money with your spouse during at least 25+ years of unemployment, or old age, so you will be able to survive, adapt to changing circumstances and live a good life.

To produce an income of $200k, for example, you will need $5mm saved and invested passively, or 25x the amount of income you and your spouse require.

Your *"Income Gap"* is the difference between your current income and the amount you really need to be earning in order to continue to afford your "immediate expenses" *and* save enough money to bridge your Savings Gap before your 60th birthday.

What is your *mood* about your Savings and Income Gaps, if you have them? Is it hopeless or possible? Are you enthusiastic or resigned?

* * * * *

5. What financial, career and business ***intentions,*** such as increasing revenues, building your identities or designing a competitive strategy, are you working to fulfill now?

> In what ways, if any, are they "strategic", or coherent with executing The Strategy effectively, strategically and competitively enough *to fulfill your ultimate financial intentions by age 60, or to have about $5m saved by then in today's dollars?*

> In what ways, if any, are they leading you to build a "Hot Dog Stand" (Book Two, Chapter 6, Part #11), which means that even if you succeed you will fail, or thwart your ultimate financial intentions to have enough money saved to avoid running out of it with your spouse before you die?

> IR#3 business philosophy is not "strategic", resulting in financial, career and business *intentions* when first learning "Aji" that are shallow, immediate and task-oriented.

> Use what you learn from the book to redesign them.

Just as often, to formulate their ambitions IR#3 businesspeople listen to "carnies" -- politicians, reporters, advertisers, academics and intellectuals -- whose advice is incompetent and disingenuous.

Instead of thinking it's important, a privilege and an honor to earn and save enough money to avoid running out of it with their spouse, who is trusting them to keep their vows,

> ... they want to first save the world, make an impact and do what they love,

> ... as if their spouse and children don't matter or don't exist.

They think making money is crass, something to feel guilty about or unbecoming. They are naïve enough to believe the "carnies" will take care of them, or even think about them, when they run out of money and are no longer useful.

6. What learning, communication, coordination and/or production *projects,* such as designing fresh, new *offers, practices, narratives* and *strategies* -- including goods and services -- are you working to fulfill effectively, strategically and competitively right now, and for the year?

> If you complete your projects will they enable you to fulfill your ultimate or final financial intentions by age 60, or are they directing you to build a "Hot Dog Stand" that is certain to thwart your intentions even if you succeed?

> If fulfilling them is not coherent with your ultimate financial intentions, redesign them if you can now and write them down.

C. *Complete last week's assignment*

7. What have you accomplished this week as a result of last week's assignment, or any past assignment?

   Have you increased your productivity, value or income?

   Has anyone noticed out loud that they are increasing?

   Are you satisfied with your accomplishments? Why, or why not?

   Do you have anything else to say about last week's assignment's meaning, relevance, value and/or purposes, or any new financial, career and business intentions?

D. The Aji Source Fundamental Strategy

8. Write down all 12 parts of The Strategy. Do this every week for 24 weeks.

> Include each part's descriptions, meanings, relevance, value and purposes.

> Allow your interpretations of each part to evolve and deepen each time you write them down.

> If you can't write The Strategy down easily, fluently and effectively, you don't know it.

> If you can't think with it while making a presentation, while answering a customer's demanding questions or when designing a new business narrative, you don't know it well enough.

> When you can speak and write The Strategy's 12 parts (1) *easily*, (2) *effectively* and (3) *fluently*, you can begin to teach it and build your networks.

E. Reading Questions

Answer these questions to develop your ability to think and act effectively, strategically and competitively when you are learning autonomously to increase your competitive capabilities, or "relative power", in the marketplace.

I recommend you read and work with the books in the order I wrote them. I wrote them to unfold gradually so new philosophical and business distinctions, concepts and practices are introduced and explained as you need them.

If you are invited into a network that is already working with "Aji", though, you may have to start at Chapter Five (Book Two), which is Week #13 in *the 24-week pivot plan*, and catch up with the rest later.

9. What opinions, assessments and/or beliefs do you already have about the reading you will do in the book this week?

Make a list of them.

For instance,

Will "Aji" really help you double your productivity, value and income?

Are you cynical, trusting or prudent?

Can you see how "Aji" is helping you pivot how you think and act in the marketplace?

Will it change how you "use" your computer and the internet?

(What do you say? What's your presupposition?)

In rapidly changing competitive situations and when learning a new business philosophy, you and everyone in your networks of colleagues, customers, employees, employers and vendors will *always* anticipate what they will read, learn, see, experience, etc.

What and how you anticipate *always* opens and closes possibilities for thought and action with what you are about to read or learn.

Learn to notice, observe and assess your predispositions, and those of your colleagues, customers, employees, employers and vendors, *before* you begin to work, think or act. It'll open your opportunities and keep them open in rapid change.

Answer these questions after *reading whatever section of the book you are learning now.*

10. What human, financial, career and business (1) *concerns,* (2) *situations,* (3) *capabilities* and (4) *strategies* (action plans) are you working on, or worried about, right now after you read the text you chose to work with this week?

   Make a list of them.

   Human concerns include housing, transportation, food and medical care, which are the most expensive and essential, by far, as well as family, play, dignity and spirituality.

   Financial concerns include how much income and savings you really need to retire (savings needs to be 25x the income you need),

      ... how quickly invested savings will grow (8%),

      ... how much inflation will reduce its value (3%),

      ... and the maximum you can withdraw annually without running out of money (4%).

Career concerns, which are "Aji", include ambitions, philosophies, strategic knowledge, Ethics of Power, How to design offers, practices, narratives and strategies (OPNS), Networks of Capabilities, autonomies, accomplishments, identities, leadership roles and anticipations.

Business concerns include constituting your fundamental offer, strategy, capital structures, selling, managing, leading, designing fresh new OPNS and profits.

11. What new "domains of thought, language and action" are opened for you when you read the text?

Make a list of them.

A "domain" is a different and more practical way of thinking about thought and action.

Each one of the following, for example, is a "domain". Each one uses different words and concepts, and is its own language, e.g., medicine, marketing, law, accounting, engineering, butterfly collecting, marriage, playing the trombone or fashion.

Each one is so easy to discern no one ever confuses them. They just don't call them "domains".

Different "domains" of thought, language and action are incredibly easy and obvious to distinguish, or locate, once businesspeople learn "Aji" and begin to listen for them.

In IR#4, learning to notice, observe and assess them is an essential "Source of Power". (Part #2)

Selling and accounting, for instance, are different "domains of language and action" because they have different *intentions* and use different *linguistic distinctions* that belong to them.

A "buying signal", for example, exists in the domain of selling while profits and losses belong in the domain of accounting.

When you are reading about operational coherence in Chapter Three or the importance of identities in Chapter Four, Difference #6, you are reading about different "domains of language and action" that did not exist in IR#3.

I wrote about them to introduce new language and explain what it means, why it is relevant, how it is valuable and why it is "on purpose" for fulfilling your intentions.

> * Chapters Three and Four are in Book One of this series.

Learning to distinguish "domains of language and action", rather than watching how people move is a powerful competitive capability. It enables IR#4 businesspeople to compete successfully in rapidly changing competitive situations.

> One way to know someone is playing baseball, for example, is by watching what they are doing, or how they are moving when they swing the bat or catch the ball.

> Another way to know the same truth is by listening to what they are saying. If people are talking about going to bat, throwing opponents out, sliding into bases and playing first base or outfield, we know they are playing baseball.

Now consider this. Is it more competitive to watch players very carefully to look for changes in their competitive capabilities and then try to figure them out and adapt to them,

> … or to listen to what they are saying to one another about how they intend to change their *ambitions, moods, language, distinctions, interpretations, intentions, commitments, practices* and *outcomes*?

What really changes in IR#4's rapidly changing competitive situations long before we can see what competitors are *doing*, although that does change,

> … is their *language, distinctions, interpretations, intentions, etc.*

They change as new offers, practices, narratives and strategies they and others produce come into existence, and long before we can see the outcomes that result.

The better you become "listening" to how domains of language change in the marketplace, including online, the better you become coping with change effectively, strategically and competitively enough to fulfill your intentions.

It will also help you know which of the more than 600,000 productivity and business applications to buy and use to fulfill your intentions, and why, so you don't have to learn all of them.

Computers and the internet are *not* changing the marketplace rapidly. People who use them effectively, strategically and competitively are, as you are learning to do with "Aji".

Languaging new strategic and competitive ideas, distinctions and practices brings them into existence for you so you can use them. This is "Aji".

"Aji" is a new domain of language and action.

It enables businesspeople and entire business organizations to increase their productivity, value and incomes so they can earn a living or become rich in IR#4.

You'll do the same for your Networks of Capabilities as you design fresh, new offers, practices, narratives and strategies.

12. What new "distinctions", words or phrases, such as marginal utilities, autonomies, descriptions, meanings, relevance, value and purposes (DMRVP), or moods, did you learn in your reading that you can use to increase your competitive capabilities, productivity, value and income tomorrow?

Make a list of them.

13. What new strategic and competitive conversations about making money to fulfill your intentions, or competing successfully, can you now have with yourself -- or your colleagues, employees, employers, customers or vendors -- as a result of your reading?

Make a list of them.

14. List 4-7 negative assessments you make about yourself, or that you made while you were reading, about your abilities to think and act effectively, strategically and competitively in the domain you were just reading about.

Make a list of them.

Everyone makes negative assessments of themselves whenever they encounter anything new they need to learn.

This includes everyone in your networks, or every colleague, customer, employee, employer and vendor with whom you work.

The purpose of this question is to reveal the negative assessments you have about yourself in this domain of action so that you can begin to anticipate them and to help you begin to see the same thing happens with everyone else.

For instance, when reading Chapter Six, Part #10: Hold highly compensated leadership roles (Book Two), you might fret that you were not born to lead and have always felt awkward standing up in front of people speaking with authority.

15. Are each of your negative assessments, or characterizations, about yourself "grounded"?

> When your assessments are "grounded" you will be able to point to evidence, or outcomes, that you are using to form your interpretation.
>
> When they are "ungrounded" you will find no evidence to support your claims, which means they are "opinions", or your psychology, not assessments.
>
> You get *practical* help to "fix" those that are grounded and *psychological* help to "let go" of, or resolve, those that are not. (Make sure you get whatever help you need now. Don't wait. *Always* move first, fast and persistently when you are competing.)

* * * * *

F. Completion Questions

16. Write 1-3 paragraphs -- at least -- that summarize what you have learned from your reading and how you will begin using it tomorrow to help you fulfill your financial, career and/or business intentions.

Write in a mood of ambition and peace to open your possibilities and opportunities to fulfill your intentions.

Don't rush. Writing helps you develop your *ambitions, moods, language, distinctions, interpretations, intentions, commitments, practices* and *outcomes*.

Don't be self-conscious when you write. Bad grammar and incomplete sentences are fine. They clear up over time.

What's important is that you write and think until you are complete and ready to think and act in new ways.

Use your writing to develop your thinking. Enjoy "becoming" a different thinker every day, rather than being, thinking and acting the same way, which is boring and uncompetitive in IR#4.

Focus on fulfilling your intentions effectively, strategically and competitively. That's "Aji".

Use what you write to bring your intentions, assessments and commitments into existence so that you can think and act with them immediately.

Use it to design, learn and develop your ability to think and act competitively so you can earn a living, or become rich.

17. What is your mood as you finish writing?

What, if anything, do you learn from this that will affect how you think and act in the future?

18. What is your assessment of *your* seriousness and adult dignity -- your integrity and value -- as you complete this week's assignment?

Are you satisfied with your work?

Did you read, write, think and speak seriously?

Were your thoughts and actions as you worked coherent with your ambitions and dignity?

Did you suffer at all when you were working?

Do you need help? (Use your networks, the internet or aji.com to find it.)

*****

* * * * *

Aji Assignment Instructions

For Building Networks of Capabilities

If you are using the book to learn "Aji" and build your Networks of Capabilities to fulfill your financial, career and business intentions with weekly meetings, you are making a "full move".

I recommend strongly that you do this:

1. Have everyone work on the same Aji Assignment for Individuals to prepare themselves for each weekly meeting.

2. Use the assignments in your meetings.

3. Start with 90-minute meetings and adjust as your knowledge grows and deepens.

* * * * *

Using the Book to Build Networks of Capabilities

Businesspeople who learn "Aji" from me report that their colleagues, customers, employers, etc., notice their productivity and value increasing in about 100 days.

> This is when IR#4 businesspeople usually begin to have enough skill designing fresh, new offers, practices, narratives and strategies to build their Networks of Capabilities.

> But the ability to begin to build a competitive network can take up to a year to develop depending upon the businessperson and the circumstances in which they work.

Building competitive "Networks of Capabilities" begins The Strategy's Strategic Pivot and along with using these assignments to learn "Aji" increases businesspeople's productivity, value and incomes immediately. (Part #6)

> This is important because before businesspeople can build competitive networks they remain isolated and too weak in a practical sense to think or act strategically and competitively enough to fulfill their financial, career and business intentions in IR#4.

>> IR#3 businesspeople work with *Networks of* **Convenience** to keep their costs low, get non-competitive help and avoid discomfort in order to "get the job done".

>>> In them businesspeople refuse pridefully to allow anyone to affect how they think or act. Popular culture entices them into thinking they are "special", that "working alone" is cool, and that their common sense is so powerful it can figure out anything.

IR#4 businesspeople work with *Networks of* **Capabilities** to increase their competitive capabilities and advantages, productivity, value and incomes every day, all day.

They listen very, very, very carefully, and respectfully, to anyone who is earning a living, or becoming rich. They are eager to learn how to think and act more effectively, strategically and competitively from dignified businesspeople who know what they're doing.

It's part of their dignity.

At the same time, IR#4 businesspeople quit listening to carnies, educators, consultants or advisors when they lack dignity because they have no proof they know what they're talking about.

Instead, they have strong opinions and speak with conviction and certainty about business, and how to make money or operate a business, but haven't produced the high IR#4 Incomes to prove the value of what they say.

Business owners, executives and managers

If you intend to "pivot" your business organization towards IR#4 you can do it two ways:

1. You can *invite* colleagues, employees, employers, vendors and customers to join you reading and using the book for the same reasons you are learning "Aji", to fulfill your financial, career and business intentions.

    I recommend this course of action when you are learning "Aji" yourself with a mix of businesspeople inside and outside your business organization.

2. You can *mandate* the pivot and drive the learning with weekly meetings and incentive compensation that recognizes increases in productivity and value they produce with the fresh, new offers, practices, narratives and strategies they learn to design.

    I recommend this course of action only after you have learned "Aji", have a Network of Capabilities and can execute The Strategy easily, effectively and fluently.

Ethics of Power and Networks of Capabilities

"Aji's" IR#4 Ethics of Power replace IR#3's labor-based and task-oriented "work ethics".

> You will learn about them in Chapter Four (Book One) and Chapter Six (Book Two).

This means you are going to start building your Networks of Capabilities before you have studied "Aji" or learned how to execute The Strategy.

> This is a real challenge that most businesspeople report is also a lot of fun because of all the unexpected difficulties they have explaining what they are talking about. They just have to laugh.

> Inviting people is not simple or easy because it requires you to know what you are doing and why you are learning "Aji". Everyone you invite is going to ask you. If your response isn't simple, seductive and compelling, they are likely to decline.

>> Most businesspeople can't begin to invite others successfully until they complete Part #1 of The Strategy: Constitute *satisfactory* Life, Financial and Business Ambitions and then have some time to practice.

***To invite people who would be useful in your network and save
yourself trouble,***

> … I suggest you have them read ***From the Author*** and ***the first
> two chapters of Book One*** before you meet with them to
> invite them to work with the book with you.

> Their interpretations and declarations will reveal their
> financial, career and business intentions.

The second challenge is running your weekly meetings so they are
valuable enough to be worth the cost of preparing and attending
them.

> IR#4 Networks of *Capabilities* are serious and transactional.
> They are informal and friendly but they are not casual. Their
> purpose is to increase everyone's strategic and competitive
> capabilities.

> People exchange help with colleagues, employees, employers,
> vendors and/or customers that is worth the cost of participating.
> This requires preparation.

> Dignified IR#4 businesspeople who work together to increase
> their competitive capabilities are not organized around their
> *convenience*, or to keep their costs low, as are IR#3's networks.
> They are organized around producing very high returns, or
> increases in competitive capabilities and advantages,
> productivity, value and incomes.

Since you will be reading and using Ethics of Power from the book, I'll present the ethics to use in your weekly meetings as simple rules.

#1 - Your Network of Capabilities (NWC) is *yours*. It isn't a club. Own it.

Building and using these networks is a strategic and competitive idea made possible by computers and the internet. They couldn't exist in IR#3.

Your NWC is the group of *colleagues, employees, employers, vendors* and *customers* with whom you work to execute The Strategy in order to fulfill your financial, career and business intentions.

People in your NWC won't know they are in "your network", nor will they care anymore than you will care about being in "their network".

#2 - Look for about a half-dozen businesspeople to read, write, speak, learn and act with as you read and use the book.

They need to be serious, ambitious and dignified.

They *don't* need to be local or convenient. They can be anywhere in the world. They work to increase your capabilities to learn, think and act with the most powerful businesspeople you can find to work and learn with.

> Working with a network frees you from being forced to work with IR#3 businesspeople around you who are cynical and/or lack ambitions, and who decline to adapt or learn.

> It frees you to design and use new *ambitions, moods, language, interpretations, distinctions, intentions, commitments, practices* and *outcomes* to produce high IR#4 Incomes that IR#3 businesspeople will not learn.

You will probably need some local members but the more businesspeople you can meet and work with who know "Aji" anywhere in the world, the better. We know, for example, that "Aji" works very well in India, Shanghai, Europe, Canada and Mexico.

> Spread out your network to build and extend your competitive capabilities.

People in your networks don't have to be in your industry or hold the same roles. You will all learn and use the same fundamental strategic knowledge to design your OPNS, build your Networks of Capabilities and produce high IR#4 Incomes. They need to share your intentions to earn a high IR#4 Income and use "Aji".

Diversity is a practical competitive advantage in "Aji" and not political.

Having NWC spread around the world, or at least the country, increases your freedom, strategic opportunities and competitive capabilities enormously and in ways IR#3 businesspeople cannot imagine.

Have businesspeople you'd like to invite to join you read **From the Author** *and* **Chapters One and Two** *in Book One before you meet with them.*

Their reactions, interpretations and commitments will help you assess whether their intentions, seriousness and dignity are appropriate.

If you have more than a half-dozen people in your meetings, they will need to be longer than 90 minutes or you will need to work with two groups.

#3 - Be serious, respectful and dignified with your networks!
       Always.

       Be serious about using IR#4's "Ethics of Power",
       which is Part #4 of The Strategy, and avoid using
       IR#3's "work ethics".

       Avoid being casual or nonchalant about anything.

       One of the fundamental differences between IR#3 and
       IR#4 is *social*, not technological.

       Everyone has computers and can speak and work with
       anyone anywhere in the world who will accept their
       request or offer.

       It behooves you to realize the new freedom
       (autonomy) everyone has to build their networks
       anywhere in the world because they will do their best
       to join the most strategic and competitive ones
       possible.

This needs to be true for you, too!

> If you take people for granted who took the time and
> made the effort to prepare ...

> If you don't respect how serious, dignified and already
> successful they are ...

> If you are casual with your commitments and
> obligations, fail to thank them thoughtfully or decline
> to behave with dignity ...

> If you act with them as if they are IR#3's Networks of
> *Convenience* to keep *your* costs down rather than
> increase *everyone's* competitive capabilities ...

>> ... you will produce bad moods, and the most
>> serious and valuable businesspeople will quit
>> first.

IR#4's Networks of *Capabilities* are populated by
businesspeople who are serious, respectful and dignified
with their careers, families, finances and one another
because the outcomes they produce matter to them.

When businesspeople don't quit networks that are not
serious and dignified, or that are casual, mediocre and
uncompetitive, because they enjoy the company,
entertainment and prestige of belonging to a business
group,

> ... the networks become pretentious social clubs, and
> no one increases their competitive capabilities or
> incomes.

What does it mean to be serious, respectful and dignified?

When you are *"serious"* you will always be careful, earnest and thoughtful about your financial situation, future intentions and networks. You'll never be casual about keeping your commitments or improving the value of what you produce.

Put the other way, how can we think adults are serious about living a good life when they are clueless about their household finances, or how much money they need to save for their old age to take care of their spouse?

(Whether a spouse works, or not, is irrelevant, yes? The concerns, obligations and consequences of failing remain the same.)

When you are *"respectful"* you will *organize how you think and act around* the concerns, situations, capabilities and strategies of the marketplace and your networks.

You will be on time, *always*.

You will have your individual assignment done thoroughly and completely for each meeting, *always*.

You will be "on purpose" in the meeting, *always*.

Being serious about your commitments to learn and be of value to others is *your* dignity in IR#4.

When you are *"dignified"* you think and act with *integrity* and *value*, which means you:

Keep your commitments

Accept the truth about your financial situation and IR#4 financial obligations

Act with humility and coherently with reality's operations,

Help those who help you take care of their concerns

When businesspeople lack ambition, seriousness, dignity and are disrespectful, they feel entitled to decline to take other people's intentions, concerns or situations seriously.

They have the right from their point of view to be casual about keeping their commitments, to have their excuses or apologies accepted without consequence and to not care about how their actions affect other people's situations.

This is how IR#3's Networks of *Convenience* work.

Think of it this way. When you have a meeting with people you respect you do not think you are entitled to waste their time, even one second of it. It's *their* life and not *yours* to waste! (And everyone always, already, knows it.)

> Being late in IR#4 for one's Networks of Capabilities, or failing to prepare, is undignified, ruins people's moods and reduces their "relative power" in the marketplace, which serious competitors will not tolerate.

> It is a display of incompetence because it shows businesspeople are *ineffective, not serious and cannot keep their commitments.*

> It is also disrespectful because it shows a lack of concern and interest in the practical value of people who have prepared for the meeting and know what *they* care about.

The same thing holds with doing your individual assignments. If you are not prepared, you will not be able to help anyone else in the meeting think or act more effectively, strategically and competitively.

> If you can't help IR#4 businesspeople in your meetings at least as much as they help you to increase your competitive capabilities and income, they can and should quit.

And, when people waste time "chatting" about what they did over the weekend, the latest technology, the political issue of the month, the new movie they saw or their excitement about an upcoming sports event,

> … instead of being "on purpose" every second of the meeting,

> … they let people know they are not serious, respectful or dignified.

Serious, dignified IR#4 businesspeople will quit them fast.

Don't confuse how IR#3 businesspeople behave with Networks of Convenience *and the way IR#4 businesspeople behave with their Networks of* Capabilities.

> They fulfill completely different intentions and require completely different skills and social practices.

*****

Assignment Questions

For Building Networks of Capabilities

A. *Always manage your moods first.*

1. Have everyone share the moods in which they found themselves *before, during* and *after* they did their individual assignment.

> *What did everyone notice, observe and assess about their moods?*

> What else has everyone noticed about moods at work that predetermine, shape and limit effective, strategic and competitive thought and action? Can they "listen" them when people speak?

> And, what are the moods of those with whom you work?

>> Are they serious about earning a living and taking care of their families?

>> Are they in "good" or "bad" moods for strategic and competitive thinking in rapid change? Why?

Examples of "bad moods" include:

> skeptical, cynical, distrustful, in despair, resigned, panicked, entitled, deserving, greedy, wonderful, naïve, opportunistic, argumentative, opining, small-minded, closed-minded, prideful, arrogant, conceited, trivializing, petty, "shitty", mean-spirited, positional and rigid.

Examples of "good moods" include:

> ambitious, dignified, curious, in wonder, interested, resolute, serious, enthusiastic and passionate.

Which moods "work" to build competitive capabilities and advantages, or to increase productivity, value and incomes when using computers and the internet, and which ones do not? Why?

> What new action will people take with their moods, and the moods of those around them, to fulfill their intentions based on what they have learned?

In the beginning, noticing and observing moods is a big challenge. As businesspeople get used to "listening" for their existence, their ability to manage their own moods, as well as those around them, gradually increases until they can do it easily, effectively and fluently.

Better moods, or ones that enable businesspeople to think and act effectively, strategically and competitively with their computers and the internet increase productivity, value and incomes.

B. *Always manage your financial, career and business intentions second*

2. Have everyone share their Life, Financial and Business Ambitions.

> Keep in mind that earning a living or becoming rich to support one's family is the most important (consequential) and dignified purpose for an adult.

> When people share, have them speak explicitly about who and what, exactly, they care about, e.g., their spouse, children, in-laws, grandchildren, society, etc. Why are they working? Why are they willing to go through all the challenges and difficulties the marketplace presents?

> When people *speak* their concerns and intentions using DMRVP, they bring them into existence. When people don't speak them, they go out of existence. It's that simple. So, talk about what's really important and why you are really working all the time.

>> Intentions and ambitions are *linguistic*, which means they only exist in people's language. They aren't like butterflies or meteors that appear to have an independent or objective existence.

> This makes knowing, speaking and sharing about one's ambitions regularly, whenever it is appropriate -- which is Part #1 of The Strategy -- essential to keeping them in existence in order to fulfill them.

>> At the same time, it helps Listeners think and reflect about theirs.

3. Have everyone share their Savings and Income Gaps and the moods their financial situation triggers, e.g., despair, hope, confidence or resolution, among others.

   If privacy is a concern, either you need to think through what harm telling the truth will cause or you have the wrong people in the group.

4. Have everyone share the financial, career and business intentions they are working to fulfill now.

   Are they working to "earn a living", or "become rich"?

   And, how much money, exactly, are they speaking about? Is it really enough?

   Are their financial numbers "straight", are they too low or too high, or are they fudging to manage their moods and psychology?

   Make sure they don't produce a Hot Dog Stand, or a situation that will fail even if they succeed.

C. The Aji Source Fundamental Strategy

5. Break into pairs and have everyone practice speaking The Strategy's 12 parts and each one's description, meanings, relevance, value and purposes until everyone can do it easily, effectively and fluently, in about 10 minutes.

> Put special attention on explaining why each part is in its location in the sequence. How does each part enable the next part?

> If you are a business owner, executive or manager, consider giving a talk using a flip chart or application so you can practice standing and writing while you talk.

6. Discuss how you can use The Strategy to ***diagnose*** your breakdowns, failures, thwarted intentions by looking *backwards*.

How is using The Strategy to diagnose and fix thwarted intentions effective, strategic and competitive?

Have everyone speak The Strategy backwards and explain how they can use each part to diagnose weaknesses in earlier parts.

7. Then discuss how you can use The Strategy to **deconstruct** what your competitors are doing by assessing how they are executing The Strategy and designing and/or executing their offers, practices, narratives and strategies, which includes their goods and services.

What are their networks, identities, highly valued accomplishments and leadership offers in the marketplace?

You can *anticipate* what they are likely to do next based on what you learned from The Strategy and IR#4 Strategic Knowledge.

Even when businesspeople don't know The Strategy, reality's operations "nudge" them to try to execute it anyway as best they can. You can exploit their weaknesses and ignorance.

Here are the three categories of competitors that drive "financial and competitive pressures" and shape standards of value your customers, employers, employees, colleagues and vendors will use to assess your offers, practices, narratives and strategies, which include your goods and services:

Primary competitors are your direct competitors whose offers, practices, narratives and strategies -- including their goods and services -- are compared directly to yours.

Secondary competitors are people making similar offers in your industry or market segment, or whose goods and services can be used as *substitutes* for yours, and who are only about two feet away from your customers on their computers all day, every day.

Tertiary competitors are competitors, especially global competitors, who drive and shape changing standards for relevance, value and purpose throughout the marketplace and whom your customers will use to judge yours. They, too, are only a couple of feet in front of your best customers.

8. Discuss how each of you is using The Strategy at work to design steady streams of fresh, new, highly valued and scarce:

Offers

Practices

Business Narratives

Strategies, or action plans

… to increase your competitive capabilities, productivity, value and incomes.

New ideas?

D. Reading Questions

9. Share with one another about the opinions, assessments and beliefs you had when you were reading the text you selected for the week.

What did you learn about your assumptions that was effective, strategic and competitive?

10. Share with one another the:

(1) Human, (2) financial, (3) career and (4) business

    1. Concerns

    2. Situations, or the:

        Competitive *threats* you need to avoid

        Obligations you need to fulfill to (1) keep
        your opportunities, (2) produce new
        opportunities and (3) avoid avoidable costs
        and risks

        Opportunities you need to exploit

    3. Capabilities, or skills to produce intended
    outcomes in a given set of competitive
    circumstances

    4. Competitive strategies (action plans) using The
    Strategy as a framework, or master plan

        … you are working on, or worried about, right
        now to fulfill your intentions.

Take some time to share with each other how each
of you is using "Aji" to increase your productivity,
value and incomes.

How are you using it to develop your Networks of
Capabilities, i.e., your colleagues, customers,
employees, employers and vendors?

Human concerns include housing, transportation, food and medical care, which are the most expensive and essential, by far, as well as family, play, dignity and spirituality.

Financial concerns include how much income and savings you really need to retire (savings needs to be 25x the income you need),

... how quickly invested savings will grow (8%),

... how much inflation will reduce its value (3%),

... and the maximum you can withdraw annually without running out of money (4%).

Career concerns, which are "Aji", include ambitions, philosophies, strategic knowledge, Ethics of Power, how to design OPNS, Networks of Capabilities, autonomies, accomplishments, identities, leadership roles and anticipations.

Business concerns include constituting your fundamental offer, strategy, capital structures, selling, managing, leading, designing fresh new OPNS and profits, which are The Spine.

Ethics of Power:

When you speak about worries, weaknesses, breakdowns and needing "help", you are not making requests for help from your network. That was possible in IR#3 because common sense and sharing "experience" worked.

> *Colleagues in IR#4 Networks of Capabilities are not there to advise or offer consulting help* unless *they have the accomplishments using "Aji" to prove their superior trustworthiness, value, authority and leadership in that domain.*
>
> In fact, an Ethic of Power you must honor with Networks of Capabilities is that knowledge is proven by the capability to produce outcomes.

> *To produce and maintain your dignity,* give and accept no advice in your meetings while you are learning "Aji" unless you have the outcomes that prove your knowledge is effective, strategic and competitive.
>
> Instead, speculate, reflect and consider without granting yourself, or anyone else, authority who hasn't yet produced the outcomes to prove their knowledge is real rather than their opinion.

Networks of Capabilities are not for convenient, cheap and commonsensical *mentoring or consulting* as was common in IR#3 when using single-purpose tools.

They are for learning, thinking, designing, planning and producing steady streams of fresh, new offers, practices, narratives and strategies using "Aji",

> *... which can be used* strategically *to fulfill people's financial, career and business intentions in the most rapidly changing competitive situations in history.*

To help one another learn responsibly, offer only your **"speculations without authority"** when you lack accomplishments or grounding so Listeners know you are not claiming certainty about what is forbidden, allowed and required to increase their capabilities.

> For example, instead of speaking strong "opinions" that imply businesspeople know what they are talking about before they can produce the incomes that prove they know what they are speaking about,

>> ... IR#4 businesspeople say, *"Based on what I understand, so far, I* speculate *that it* might *be more effective, strategic and competitive to (do the following)."*

11. Share the new "domains of thought and action" that were opened for you when you read the text, explanations and claims, and how you are using them to fulfill your intentions.

   Go through your lists.

12. Share the new "distinctions" you learned and found most important, useful and worthwhile, or valuable, to increase your competitive capabilities. Remember, "distinctions" are words or phrases we use to distinguish, notice, observe and assess what is in our environment and what we are experiencing.

   Go through your lists.

13. Share the new conversations you can have with yourself -- or with your colleagues, employees, employers, customers or vendors -- to produce competitive advantages by increasing your competitive capabilities, productivity, value and income as a result of your reading.

   Go through your lists.

14. Share the 4-7 negative assessments you made about yourself and about your abilities to think and act effectively, strategically and competitively in the domain you were just reading about.

Go through your lists.

Were any of them grounded? How will you "fix" them?

If they were ungrounded and psychological, how will you "let go" of them, or resolve them, so you are free to think and act as you need to in order to fulfill your Life, Financial and Business Ambitions?

What are you learning? Do you need to take action? Do you need help?

E. Completion Questions

15. What are your financial, career and business intentions for the following week? What outcomes do you intend to produce?

List them.

16. How do you intend to use The Strategy and the IR#4 Strategic Knowledge you just discussed tomorrow and next week to increase your productivity, value and incomes?

List them.

17. Was everyone on time and ready to go at the meetings announced start time and not even one second late?

Did everyone complete their individual assignments?

Was everyone "on purpose" the entire time so there were no irrelevant conversations, even for one second?

Any complaints, suggestions or requests?

18. Are *you* satisfied with the competitive capabilities, dignity and seriousness of each person in your network?

If not, what actions will you take to continue building your Networks of Capabilities to open your strategic and competitive opportunities?

19. Are *they* satisfied with *your* seriousness, discipline, dignity and respect for everyone else?

Check to see if they agree.

Listen carefully to any negative assessments and/or requests for you to improve how you learn, communicate, coordinate thought and action and/or help them produce fresh, new, highly valued and scarce offers, practices, narratives and strategies they can use to fulfill their intentions.

*****

How to Learn ... Anything

Recurrence, Reciprocation and Recursion

Whenever I first work with businesspeople about learning "Aji", especially when I am selling, most of them have had such terrible experiences in school they can barely hear what I am saying. They don't want to "be taught" like that again.

Schooling children has been turned over to the government, which is coercive. That's all governments of any kind know, no matter what they say. The only other way to be of service with an offer such as schooling is to have people accept it as valuable enough that they do not need to be coerced. Politicians can't and won't do this.

This means most businesspeople I've met associate "learning" with "being taught" under the duress of a teacher who passed a test to get their credential from the government but who doesn't usually use what they teach in real life.

Consequently, when we are children we get taught math, writing and history by adults who don't actually use the math, writing or history they teach in the world themselves, which is absurd and shows up in the way they "teach".

Being taught as a child by being threatened by adults in order to "learn",

... and *learning* how to fulfill one's most important, cherished and dignified obligations voluntarily, enthusiastically and passionately,

... are not in the same universe of experiences.

Learning seriously as an adult, enthusiastically and with dignity to take care of our family is work, to be sure, but it is also joyful, deeply meaningful, creative, inspiring and to those of us who really enjoy competing to make money, it is Kick-Ass Wonderful!

Below are the "keys to the domain" of one of the most strategic and competitive practices needed to compete successfully in IR#4 to earn a living or become rich, "autonomous competitive learning". (To refresh yourself on the practice, see Chapter Four, Difference #2 in Book One.)

Using this practice for the rest of your career enables you to learn whatever and whenever you want or need to in order to fulfill your financial, career and business intentions in IR#4's rapidly changing competitive situations.

This is raw competitive power that is made possible by computers and the internet. IR#3 businesspeople could not practice autonomous competitive learning with their single-purpose tools.

It creates a new way to use your computers and the internet to increase your competitive capabilities and advantages, productivity, value and incomes ... whenever you need or want to.

Imagine. If you find something "interesting" that might be highly valued and scarce relative to demand while you are reading this book you can go online to learn about it.

Imagine. If it occurs to you that there might be a few other businesspeople "online" who know "Aji", or who are using the book to learn it, you can go online and find them.

The "keys to the domain" of autonomous competitive learning are the three practices of recurrence, reciprocation and recursion.

These practices are simple and straightforward to learn.

Once you get the hang of the three practices, you can learn and/or teach "anything" that is possible to learn or teach, including "Aji".

Whether online or in your groups learning "Aji", if you start discussing a better way to design your offers so they are more competitive and valuable, you'll know how to *learn* what you did without being taught using the three practices.

And you can do it your own way because there are as many ways to use the three practices as you can imagine.

They work underwater because I used them to learn how to scuba dive.

They work in planes.

They work in meetings, sales presentations, accounting classes, manufacturing departments, etc.

I also recommend you pay close attention to the character of the people with whom you learn in your networks.

People aren't things. Everyone is different. There are many ways businesspeople think and act with dignity ... and learn.

NWC are not clubs and no one is entitled to join yours, ever. People earn their place happily and eagerly, or they don't belong.

There are also many ways businesspeople who are jerks, bullshitters and frauds pretend they are dignified adults to avoid costs without being discovered. *They are easy to spot with "Aji".*

They won't do the reading, complete the assignments or constitute their financial ambitions with their spouse.

They are not committed to learning what they need to in order to earn a living or become rich in IR#4.

So, who will you invite who is serious, dignified and competent enough to be of real strategic and competitive help if they learned "Aji"?

My final recommendation is that you design the different ways you *learn* "Aji", and do the assignments so that they are part of what you call living a good life.

You'll have to design your learning practices gradually as you learn how to learn and discover what works best for you. Allow your practices to unfold and change as it suits you.

Take your time inventing your learning practices and speak about them with your networks as you learn. Doing this will change your life, career, business and finances in IR#4.

*****

How to Learn ... Anything

Recurrence, Reciprocation and Recursion

In IR#4's rapidly changing competitive situations you will have to learn about new offers, practices, narratives and strategies (OPNS) that appear from many sources all day, every day.

To learn, or to have your Networks of Capabilities learn (1) *easily*, (2) *effectively* and (3) *fluently,* you use the following three learning practices every day, all day.

These three practices -- *recurrence, reciprocation and recursion* -- are all you need to learn in order to learn anything, or to have your networks learn.

You will use them for the rest of your career because they are effective, strategic and competitive.

> They enable you to compete in rapidly changing, complex, intensely competitive and technologically advanced competitive situations.

Recurrence   means to *revisit* an intention or practice to fulfill that intention regularly.

To practice "recurrence", IR#4 businesspeople revisit their ambitions, intentions and knowledge regularly and often by *talking* and *writing* about them in as many different ways that are effective, strategic and competitive as possible.

People often confuse repetition and recurrence.

When we repeat something we intend to perform the same movements or actions over and over again, which is impossible because our bodies and the situations in which we find ourselves practicing or learning are always changing.

Our bodies do not like repetition. It makes us dull and uncomfortable.

Recurrence is not the same as repetition, and it requires us to be alert and produce the recurrence deliberately.

Our nervous systems like recurrence. It stimulates and energizes our thoughts and actions.

To practice recurrence we "revisit" intentions and actions throughout the day, every day, by speaking about them and using them in different situations and to fulfill slightly different intentions. This drives our nervous system to continually adjust and learn, *and it feels good.*

Think of learning to play golf. If beginners go to the driving range and practice the same swing over and over, again, they don't learn much because their body, or their nervous system, doesn't respond well to *repetition*.

But, if they only spend a short time on the driving range warming up and reorienting themselves,

> ... and then start practicing their swing by using it in different situations to avoid different threats, fulfill different obligations and exploit different opportunities,

> ... *they learn much more quickly and enjoy learning much more, too.*

Learning with recurrence is more like play and inventing fun than it is academic studying to pass tests in school.

It changes everyone's moods to enthusiasm about learning, and passion for the future they are creating, at the same time it makes them more productive and valuable.

Reciprocation   means to *respond*, or to *notice and observe a response* businesspeople produce with how they speak and/or act in the marketplace.

Businesspeople produce "reciprocation" two ways:

They produce it *individually* by noticing the outcomes they produce with their actions in the physical world. Think of practicing tennis by hitting the ball against a wall to see outcomes from different swings.

They produce it *socially* by noticing the interpretations, commitments and actions they trigger when they make offers, perform practices, speak business narratives or design and execute action plans.

To practice "reciprocation" IR#4 businesspeople *dance* through the marketplace with people and artifacts while *noticing* and *observing* how and why everything they say and every action they perform creates corresponding actions and movements in response, *or outcomes.*

* * * * *

Recursion   means to refer back to itself for meaning, relevance, value and purpose.

It is the *practice* of reflecting on, or making effective, strategic and competitive *interpretations* about the:

> *Outcomes* that are produced
>
> *Narratives* and *practices* used to produce them
>
> *Circumstances* -- threats, obligations and opportunities -- in which thought and action occurred

Recursion enables you to deepen and better understand (1) *what* you are doing, (2) *why* you are producing the outcomes you do and (3) *what* you need to do to better fulfill your intentions.

Noticing "recursion", and practicing it, is often difficult, at first, even though we all practice recursion every day as we encounter the same concerns, situations, capabilities and strategies throughout the day, or ones that are similar to them.

We deepen our understanding of them,

> … if we *reflect* on the outcomes we've noticed and observed individually or with others,
>
> … and combine our reflections with our already existing knowledge and that of others to produce new interpretations of how to improve them.

The aim of recursion, or reflection after thought and action, is to improve narratives, outcomes, practices and circumstances so that they are more (1) effective, (2) strategic and (3) competitive, and in this order.

Think of learning to play golf, again. When we are beginners we are, by definition, incompetent, which means we are unable to act and fulfill our intentions in a given set of circumstances.

We "learn" how to become competent by learning a method to perform a practice we trust works, such as how to swing a golf club properly or how to design a fresh new offer, and by trying to "perform" it to fulfill our intentions as many times as we need to until we can produce the outcomes we intend.

This is *recurrence.*

This produces a real opportunity to use our understanding of a golf swing on the course to *notice* and *observe* the *outcomes* our swings produce -- individually or socially -- so that we can assess and improve them.

This is *reciprocation.*

The trick is to then assess one's (1) *outcomes* and the (2) *narratives* and (3) *practices* used to produce them, as well as the (4) *circumstances* in which we are acting in order to improve their value by redesigning them or improving execution. We also do this individually or with others.

This is *recursion.*

"Aji" enables this, as you will see.

IR#4 businesspeople practice recurrence, reciprocation and recursion with each other throughout the day,

    ... because using all three is required to learn.

They practice their learning skills by performing or speaking them to continually build their "backgrounds", interpretations and skills.

Using all three learning skills produces a "virtuous circle" of power, or continuous learning, that enables businesspeople to build their strategic knowledge and competitive capabilities throughout the day to fulfill their financial, career and business intentions.

As businesspeople use "Aji" their ability to use all three fundamental learning practices with their Networks of Capabilities -- their colleagues, employees, employers, vendors and customers -- steadily increases.

*****

* * * * *

Manage your moods when you learn The Strategy

IR#4 businesspeople always work with their moods first because moods *predetermine* what they and their networks of colleagues, employees, employers, customers and vendors are willing to think about or do. People's moods *predetermine* what thoughts and actions are possible, or impossible.

> For instance, do people who are deeply sad at a funeral ever think to balance their checkbook or invite people to their birthday party during the ceremony?

> Do businesspeople who are working hard with determination and who are busy completing tasks ever think to stop and learn a new strategy or design a fresh, new offer with a colleague?

Avoid being distrustful, argumentative or cynical for no reason.

> In other words, stop declining requests to learn!

> Declines to adapt to existing competitive and technological circumstances in order to increase productivity, value and incomes are "bad moods" in IR#4.

> They shut down your willingness to accept help; are insulting and costly to your colleagues; and encourage those who can help you, to make their offers to others instead.

It's ok to be interested and even enthusiastic about learning new distinctions, intentions and practices to earn a living or become rich to take care of your spouse, children and yourself.

The fun and stimulation many businesspeople experience when they learn "Aji" often catch them by surprise.

Many businesspeople find it refreshing to design new offers, practices, narratives and strategies (OPNS) of their own and to make money with them directly, rather than by proxy, e.g., spending hours working hard and keeping busy.

Be in a good mood and unapologetically serious about your life, marriage and children when you learn.

Never, ever, be in a task-oriented mood that makes you "too busy" to learn. It will thwart your intentions to earn a living or become rich. Good moods about learning are needed to attract and build competitive Networks of Capabilities, and to become rich in IR#4.

It's worth saying, again, to make enough money to live a good life with your family,

… *stop* declining requests to learn and adapt to increase your productivity, value and income.

Make sure your moods of *ambition, humility, wonder, enthusiasm, passion* and *gratitude,* explained below, are established in your body before you learn with your "Aji Group" or your potential Network of Capabilities.

If you are a business owner, executive or manager, make sure your colleagues, employees, employers, vendors or customers are in these moods before you teach them The Strategy.

Here are brief descriptions of each **mood** needed to compete
successfully in IR#4 competitive situations using computers, the
internet and Networks of Capabilities:

Ambition   Hold deeply meaningful commitments to produce
                    future financial situations in which you and your
                    spouse can survive, adapt to life's always changing
                    circumstances and live a good life until you are at
                    least 90 years old -- the most important and
                    dignified commitments adults make.

                    Allow yourself to remember that making "enough
                    money" in IR#4 has a *new meaning. It now includes
                    having to save enough money to afford 25+ years of
                    old age with your spouse.*

                    Failing or declining to earn a living triggers serious,
                    harsh and life-threatening consequences for your
                    spouse, children, in-laws, grandchildren and you.

Being unapologetically serious about fulfilling your ambitions
to produce "adult dignity", instead of being indifferent, casual
or empty-headed, makes whatever you are learning and
practicing meaningful, relevant, valuable, "on purpose" and
much more interesting for everyone.

Real life, especially fierce competition to earn a living or
become rich, is never academic, intellectual, comfortable, neat
and tidy, easy or obvious. It's *practical, inconvenient, costly,
difficult as hell, and it never stops.* Competitors make sure of
this.

Humility   Modesty, a lack of pride and arrogance, and a well-grounded sense of one's actual capabilities to fulfill financial, career and business intentions in a given situation are powerful in IR#4 when used to fulfill serious, dignified and meaningful commitments to "earn a living" or become rich, and produce adult dignity.

Humility, which is (1) the absence of arrogance and pride, coupled with (2) assessments about one's relative capabilities to fulfill intentions in a context of threats, obligations and opportunities, enables businesspeople to learn, build competitive Networks of Capabilities and earn high IR#4 Incomes.

It has businesspeople realize that *giving* and *accepting strategic and competitive help* is required and dignified to compete successfully in the most rapidly changing, complex, competitive and technologically advanced global marketplace in human history.

Arrogance, pride, being cocky and defiant, and "lone rangering", on the other hand, which is promoted by popular culture and was tolerated in IR#3, shut down all willingness to learn or help others effectively, strategically and competitively.

Wonder   Marvel at all there is to learn and practice with "Aji"
                 that will help you fulfill your financial, career and
                 business intentions.

Be curious and interested, rather than certain that you already
know all there is to know that matters, even if you keep these
assessments to yourself.

Allow yourself to be amazed as you learn the new *ambitions,
moods, language, distinctions, interpretations, intentions,
commitments, practices* and *outcomes* you can produce with
your computer, the internet and networks.

Don't trivialize, be thoughtless or act with indifference when
you learn something new that will help you fulfill your most
important and dignified purpose with your family, who is
trusting you to take care of them.

Instead, express your wonder at all there is to learn that really
matters and say thank you respectfully, thoughtfully,
strategically, competitively and often to those who help you
fulfill your most important and dignified intentions.

Enthusiasm   Be eager to learn all the *practical know-how* you possibly can to increase your competitive advantages, productivity, value and income, and to perform all the actions you need to take to fulfill your ambitions every day, all day.

Passion   It's ok to be a bit over-the-top and even a little obsessed with earning a living or becoming rich when the consequence you are working to avoid is running out of money with your spouse during 25+ years of old age.

Don't be "cool" or casual about your future with your spouse and children, or pretend to be, and get a little "hot" and passionate about it, instead.

Let colleagues know how much it matters when it is appropriate. It works and it attracts networks of equally serious and passionate IR#4 businesspeople. Networks of Capabilities are always "hot" and passionate, or they fall apart.

Gratitude   Don't hold back or be stingy with your thanks and appreciation. Instead, *compete with your thanks* because identities are strategic, competitive and matter much more in IR#4.

Speaking one's gratitude thoughtfully, meaningfully and with dignity is power and money in IR#4 for the person you thank, and for you. Don't withhold it.

"Thanks" acknowledges the value of help and builds identities of *superior* trustworthiness, value, authority and leadership, which increases the "social power" of whoever you thank.

Reflect seriously about the value of the help you receive throughout the day and what the other person had to do to learn the knowledge before they could offer it. Then, for a change, gush your thanks and speak its value -- importance, utility and worth -- without trivializing it.

Don't be the smartest, all-knowing person in the room, who is critical and nit-picky automatically when you get help you really need -- even if you are only thinking it, rather than speaking it -- or you'll stop getting the help you really need.

Don't pretend you are indifferent to getting help and that you'll be "fine" financially if you don't get help when your income and savings are already too low.

Start compensating people who seriously help you, with "thank you's" that are respectful, dignified, thoughtful, strategic and competitive, and sometimes with checks. If you don't do both, you'll end up without enough money to survive, adapt and live a good life with your spouse during your old age.

*****

* * * * *

Continue to Learn and Use "Aji"

To Double Your Productivity, Value and Income

Book One

Use the *Introduction* and *Chapters One through Four* to:

Learn the Author's personal reasons for designing "Aji" and writing this book series.

See how to use the books to learn the new *strategic intentions* and *tactical business skills* required to increase your income, earn a living or become rich in IR#4.

Preview *The Aji Source Fundamental Strategy* and learn the fundamental, practical, strategic and competitive differences between IR#3 and IR#4 that make using your computers and the internet to make money meaningful, dignified and successful.

Book Two

Use *Chapter Five* to learn how The Strategy is organized, how it works, and how to use it to change your *orientation, strategic intentions* and *business skills* to increase your productivity, value and income.

Use *Chapter Six* to learn each part of The Strategy so that you can get started using "Aji" in your career and business to fulfill your financial, career and business intentions.

*****

Additional "Aji" Resources

"Aji" is rich with *IR#4 Strategic Knowledge.* We couldn't possibly fit it all into one book.

At present we have seven books and more than 1,300 papers and 400+ videos available on aji.com to help businesspeople use "Aji" to double their productivity, value and income, produce top 1% incomes, and increase the enterprise values of their businesses.

Increase your competitive capabilities and advantages to fulfill your financial, career and business intentions with "Aji" books, online resources, courses, programs and meetings, and in-person annual conferences.

Aji, An IR#4 Business Philosophy

A Three-Book Series

Book One: *"Aji"*

*The Strategic and Competitive Differences
Between IR#3 and IR#4*

Book Two: *Learning and Using "Aji" to Earn a Living or
Become Rich*

Book Three: *Assignments and Reflection Questions for
Individuals and Networks of Capabilities to Begin
to Increase Their Productivity, Value and Incomes*

* All three books are available on Amazon.

Aji Notes

Strategic Distinctions and Competitive Business Skills

To Double Productivity, Value and Income

Volumes 1 - 4

Aji Notes is a collection of the most strategic, competitive and fundamental "Aji" distinctions and practices.

The author's purpose for publishing *Aji Notes* is to enable you and your Network of Capabilities -- your employer, employees, colleagues, customers and vendors -- to learn and use the distinctions and practices easily and enjoyably to fulfill your financial, career and business intentions.

* All four volumes are available on Amazon.

Aji Online

aji.com

Following is a partial list of the always changing resources on *aji.com* you can use to increase your productivity, value and income, and that of your Networks of Capabilities.

Courses and Programs

The Introduction to Aji Course

The Aji Starter's Course

Double Your Income Subscription

Earn Top 1% Income Subscription

The Aji Intention Fulfillment Programs

Papers and Essays

The Fundamental Human Concerns and Their Existential, Strategic and Competitive Utility

The Fundamental Business Concerns and Their Financial, Strategic and Competitive Importance In IR#4

The Fundamental Marriage Concerns

The Aji Source Fundamental Strategy's 12 Strategic Intentions (The Fundamental Career Concerns)

To Design Superior Offers, Practices, Narratives and Strategies, Know Why Money Is a Fundamental Concern

Designing Offers

Value

Producing Superior Trustworthiness

What Is Meaning?

What Are Business Narratives and How Are They Organized?

Top 1% Leadership

Videos

The Aji Source Fundamental Strategy

How to Begin to Design an Offer

Trust, Sincerity, Competence and Reliability

Formulating Life, Financial and Business Ambitions Is the First Strategic Move to Get Out of the Bottom 99%

DMRVPs for Marginal Offers Must Be Spoken. They are Not Obvious.

7 Parts For How to Work With a Business Narrative

Other Subjects, for example

Human, Financial, Career and Business Concerns

*DMRVP: Descriptions, Meanings, Relevance, Value and
                   Purposes*

*Business Narratives: The Exposition, Conflict, Rising Action,
                   Resolution and Denouement*

How to Develop Networks of Capabilities

Power: Sources, Forms, Categories, Methods and Axioms

Time and "Spaces of Possibilities"

Competitive Advantages: Fundamental, Strategic and Tactical

*****

"Aji" Distinctions, Practices and Lists

In This Book Series

About The Strategy

The Aji Source Fundamental Strategy

Production, Diagnosis, Deconstruction, Anticipation

"Aji" Distinctions

Ethics and "Ethics of Power" (EoP)   108, 336 Book One

"Aji" Practices

"Aji" Lists

Ambition   122 Book Two

Commitments, Directions, Velocities and Focuses

Categories of Time for Design   464 Book Two

"Spaces of Possibilities"

CDVF   123 Book Two

Commitment, Direction, Velocity, Focus

CSCS   258 Book One

Concerns, Situations, Capabilities, Strategies

Fundamental Concerns   99, 258 Book One, aji.com

Human (13), Financial (6), Career (12, Aji), Business (22)

Fundamental Human Concerns:

Body, Family, Work, Play, Sociability, Education, Money, Career, Membership, World, Dignity, Situation, Spirituality

Identities and TVAL

Moods Needed to Compete in IR#4

OPNS

Offers, Practices, Business Narratives and Strategies

Possibilities, Impossibilities and Opportunities

Strategies

What is a Philosophy of Competition?   160 Book Two

www.ingramcontent.com/pod-product-compliance
Lightning Source LLC
Chambersburg PA
CBHW071958220326
41599CB00032BA/6428